How to Prevent the Attack of Bed bugs!

How to Prevent the Attack of Bed bugs!

MAKING YOU AND YOUR FAMILY SAFE FROM BED BUGS

Brent Youngblood and Kevin Youngblood

ISBN: 0692388273
ISBN 13: 9780692388273
Library of Congress Control Number: 2015933951
werner james publishers, millbrae, CA

Contents

How to Use This Book

If you want to learn about bedbugs and their habits, read chapter 1.
If you travel a lot, read chapter 2.
If your major concern is protecting your home and your family, read chapters 3 and 4, and get the products discussed in chapter 4.

Please note that while we are writing about an icky subject, we will try to keep the ickyness to a minimum. We did not include pictures of bedbugs. There are plenty of nasty pictures on the Internet if you want to get grossed out.
OK, let's get started!

A special thanks to Curly and Rhys, our canine inspectors. Without their devotion, work, and incredible noses, we would not have been able to write this book. They are truly man's best friend.

Introduction

Who We Are and Why We Wrote This Book for You
We wrote this book because we want to help you. We are Scent Tek, and we have been in business for over six years, using dogs to perform bedbug inspections in the San Francisco Bay Area. Since we have been in business, we have performed over seven thousand inspections for single-family homes, condos, apartments, hotels, motels, dormitories, senior-living spaces, movie theaters, restaurants, public-transportation vehicles, clothing stores, and the like. We have strong working relationships with many hotels and pest-control operators (i.e., exterminators). In addition, we are the largest independent bedbug-inspection service in the San Francisco Bay Area, and we are proud of our many five-star Yelp reviews. Over the years, we have been continually asked to give presentations about bedbugs and the value of using dogs for bedbug inspections.

Along with our six years of field experience, we have attended over six entomologist seminars and conferences on bedbugs. We are not entomologists, but we have a very good understanding of the history, biology, and behavior of bedbugs.

Based on our six years of field-inspection experience and our observations of all the different treatment strategies, we believe this book will help you to be bedbug-free in your home, today and in the future.

Our approach and philosophy is that this is a battle of the species. If you understand your opponents, you can defeat them and win!

CHAPTER 1

What You Need to Know about the Bedbug

What Are Bedbugs, and Where Did They Come From?

Bedbugs are insects, like fleas, ticks, and mites. Their sole source of food is human blood. Bedbugs evolved from bat bugs.

The theory of their evolution goes like this: when humans entered caves for shelter and built fires in them, the smoke may have driven the bats away that lived there—but not the bat bugs. Without their food source, the bat bugs found humans to be a suitable replacement, as humans and bats are both warm-blooded mammals not possessing fur.

Now let us use our imaginations. Caves are dark. Their walls are cool and offer many crevices to hide in, and if you are a bat bug, you feel safe. Bats fly out of the caves to get food and water. When they return to the caves, they land, hang from the walls, and sleep. When bats sleep, they do not move. During this time, a bat bug will crawl out of its hiding place, or harborage, climb onto a bat, and get its fill of blood. Once the bat bug is full, it will crawl off the bat and go back to hiding, somewhere very close to the sleeping bat.

OK, now that you know about the bat bug and its environment, let us look at the bedbug's environment. The following exercise might seem a little weird, but we hope it will help your understanding. Imagine you are the bat and your bedroom is a cave. Like the bat, you leave your bedroom for the day to get food and water.

What in your bedroom resembles a cave wall with crevices? Yep, it's your mattress, especially your box spring and bed frame. Your mattress offers the bedbug many hard-surfaced nooks and crannies to hide in. Now imagine it is the end of the day, and it is time for bed. You are the hairless bat going to sleep. During this period, it's dark, and you aren't moving. The bedbug crawls out of its harborage, crawls onto you, and gets its fill of blood. Once the bedbug is full, it will crawl off you and go back to hiding in a crevice very close to you.

How Do Bedbugs Find Us?

If you have a bedbug in your home, it will find you. It may take a while, but the bug *will* find you. Think of yourself as a campfire in the woods. You are stationary and giving off heat and carbon dioxide. Now, when are you most like a campfire? Yep, when you are sleeping. Thus this is when it is easiest for the bedbug to find you. When the bedbug is within about twelve feet of you, it senses your breathing vibrations. The bug thinks, "I sense a meal source, so I am going to make my way in that direction." Once the bug is within about three feet of you, it senses your carbon dioxide and body heat. The bug says, "Bingo! Found it!" Once the bug gets its fill of blood, it says, "Here is the buffet table. I think I will find a hiding place within about three feet of it." What provides a hiding place for a small bug and is almost always within three feet of where you sleep? That's right—the bed. Hence, these insects are called bedbugs.

How Do Bedbugs Get in Our Homes?

You may be wondering how bedbugs get into our living spaces? This is pretty easy to answer. Bedbugs are considered transfer pests, meaning *we* bring them into our indoor environment. Not to freak you out, but anybody coming into your home is a potential carrier of bedbugs. This includes family and friends.

Bedbugs are great hitchhikers. Unlike most pests, they don't fly in, they don't crawl in, and they don't come in on other mammals (like rats, birds, and the like). Humans carry the bugs in on luggage, backpacks, purses, computers or computer bags, used furniture, books, and clothes.

An important reminder as you read this gem of a book: the term *luggage* refers to *anything* you carry out of your home and bring back home

Where Can You Get Bedbugs?

Basically, you can pick up bedbugs in places where other people are or have been. This includes hotels, motels, lodgings, theaters, public transit, airlines, trains, cruise ships,dormitories, preschools, schools, used-furniture stores, and second-hand stores.

How Bad Can It Be If I Take No Action?

If you bring home a single male bedbug and take no action, you will get bites every three to five days for approximately eighteen months at most; then the bedbug will die of old age. If you bring home one male and one female or one inseminated female, you have a recipe for creating a great bedbug empire! In six months' time, you could have over a thousand happy bedbugs where you sleep!

Facts and Myths about Bedbugs

Facts

1. Their life expectancy is approximately eighteen months.
2. When they have a steady meal source, they feed, on average, every three to five days.
3. They can live up to four to six months without a meal.
4. Their eggs hatch in ten to fourteen days, depending on the temperature.

5. There are five life stages from egg to adult.
6. Once a female is inseminated, she can lay up to three hundred eggs for the remainder of her life. However, she needs to feed in order to lay eggs. No food source means no egg laying.
7. They typically feed at night and are generally sensitive to light.
8. They prefer to be in physical contact with other bedbugs.

Myths

1. They can live for a year or two without eating.
2. They go dormant and hibernate.
3. Pets can bring them into the home.
4. Bedbugs can jump and fly.

CHAPTER 2

What You Need to Know
When You Leave Your Home

How to Protect Yourself When Traveling

The following are simple tools and tips to use when traveling.
Travel Tools

- A flashlight for inspecting the bed
- Clothing-storage bags

Arriving at Your Lodging

- Never put your luggage on the bed.
- Store your luggage in the bathroom.
- When you first enter your room, do the following:
  - Put your luggage in the bathtub or shower.
  - Pull back the linens on the bed and check the mattress and headboard for bedbugs and bedbug fecal matter, which looks like black pepper. This process requires pulling the bed away from the wall and takes about five minutes.

What You Cannot Control

Many times, you cannot completely control the transportation of your luggage from home and back. The door to your home is the first line of defense. Upon returning home, if you are concerned about possible bedbug exposure, place your luggage in large plastic garbage bags, and tie them closed. When time permits, you can process the items before bringing them into the living areas of your home.

Remember, if the bedbugs do not make it into your living area, you have a very high probability of staying bedbug-free.

CHAPTER 3

What You Need to Do to Protect
Yourself and Your Family

When You Come Home from a
Trip, the Workplace, or a Visit

First, let's start with coming home from a trip. Upon your return
home, follow these steps:

1. Leave your luggage in the garage, landing, storage area, or
    laundry area.
2. Remove clothing from your luggage, put it in plastic bags,
    and transfer it to the washing machine.
3. Wash and dry everything on high heat for forty-five minutes.
    Bedbugs die at 122 degrees Fahrenheit.
4. Put your luggage in black plastic bags, and store it outside
    of living and sleeping areas.
5. If possible, once your luggage is in black plastic bags, put
    the bags in the sun for a couple of days. If you have a car,
    you can put the black plastic bags in the car. Then, with the
    windows rolled up, park the car in the sun for a day. Your car
    acts like an oven, and the little buggers will die in the heat
    (pun intended).
6. If the day is not warm, spray the luggage with rubbing alco-
    hol, and store it in black plastic bags.

7. Please note: whatever you put in the black plastic bags needs to get to 122 degrees or higher. If it does not, the bedbugs will survive. We suggest putting a thermomoter in the bag(s).

Upon returning from work or visiting friends or family, *never* put what you are carrying (your purse, backpack, computer, and so on) on your bed, couch, or chair. Remember that bedbugs like nooks and crannies. They will wait wherever you leave them for a human to sit or lie down. As long as you are within three feet of them, they can find you easily. They sense carbon dioxide and body heat.

The best thing you can do with any item you are carrying is to hang it up or put it in a storage container. The storage container should have very smooth interior walls, which will prevent the bed-bugs from crawling out.

How to Inspect for Bedbugs
Do-It-Yourself Inspections

- Use a bright flashlight.
- Concentrate your inspection in bedrooms and living areas where people rest or sleep.
- Look for bedbugs hiding in cracks, crevices, folds of fabric, wood, and paper items.
- Examine mattress seams, welting, and box springs.
- Dismantle and inspect bed frames, headboards, and footboards.
- Examine the top, sides, and bottom of furniture.
- Examine electrical receptacles, switch plates, thermostats, and smoke detectors.
- Look behind any art hanging on walls.
- Examine baseboards, moldings, and loose wallpaper.
- Unfasten carpeting for inspection at the baseboard, and ex-amine the length of the carpet's tack strip.

Professional Inspections

- Engage a local exterminator, who will perform a visual inspection.
- Engage a bedbug-sniffing dog team. This involves visual inspection and odor detection by a professional dog team.

How to Make Your Bed Bedbug-Proof

Even if you do nothing else described in this fabulous fountain of information (drumroll please), never put anything on your bed but yourself and your friends. To reiterate, this means no luggage, no backpacks, no computers, and no purses. Basically, beds are for humans only.

The idea is to create a bug-free sleep space by isolating the bed. We call this "bed isolation." Remember, these bugs are crawlers, not jumpers or fliers.

Follow these simple steps:

1. The bed must be on a frame, preferably one with legs. If the box spring and mattress are on the floor, any crawling bug can join you on the bed. If the mattress or box spring is on the floor, it *must* be encased.
2. Make sure the bed, pillows, and linens do not touch any wall or the floor. You only need about an inch of space between the bed and walls. Again, bedbugs are crawlers, not jumpers.
3. Encase the mattress and box spring. By doing this, you eliminate harborage opportunities. In addition, the encasements are white, which will make it easy for you to see a bug or bedbug fecal matter on them.
4. Install ClimbUp Interceptors under each leg of the bed frame. These devices are simple, easy to use, and inexpensive. If the legs are the only way for the bedbugs to get onto your bed, the bugs will get trapped in the ClimbUp Interceptors

and will not reach the bed. A bonus of ClimbUp Interceptors is that they also trap other crawling bugs, so you can be sure that you'll sleep bite-free.

5. Make sure the frame is decontaminated. You can apply alcohol to the frame, or you can steam the frame.

Here is how bed isolation works: your warm, stationary sleeping body is the bait, and the ClimbUp Interceptors are the traps. When the interceptors are installed under each leg of the bed, the bedbugs cannot crawl onto the bed. The result is no bites. With no food source, the females will stop laying eggs, and any newly hatched bugs will also be unable to feed and will die.

How to Encase Your Mattress and Box Spring
You can encase your mattress and box spring in three steps

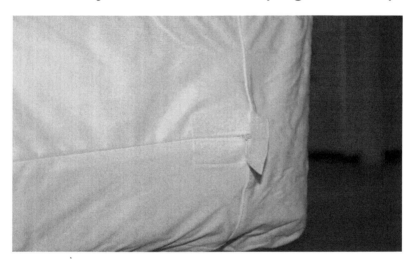

1. Install the encasement, and zip it closed.

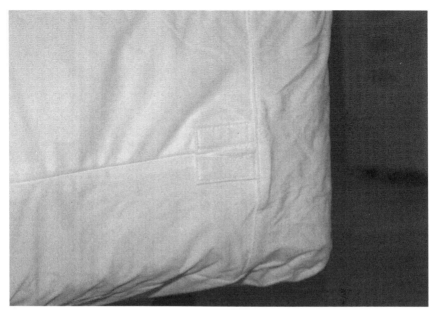

2. Secure the locking mechanism so the zipper does not open up.

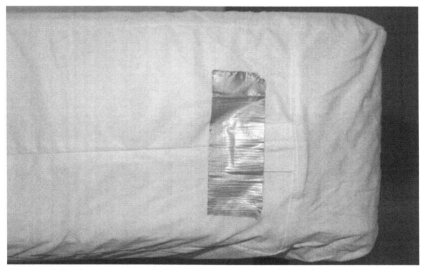

3. For added security and to prevent accidental opening, we recommend placing duct tape over the zipper enclosure.

How to Use ClimbUp Interceptors
A first step in bed isolation

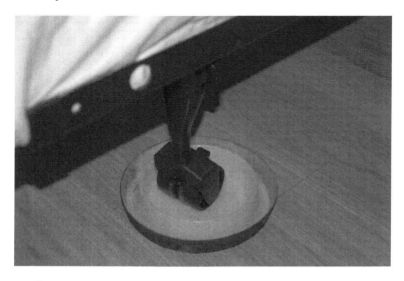

1. Install one ClimbUp Interceptor under each leg of your bed frame, the headboard, and the footboard.

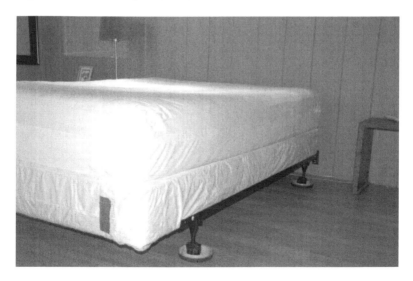

2. Make sure each leg has a ClimbUp Interceptor.

Bed Isolation

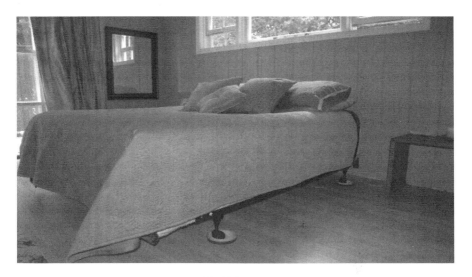

The Right Way

- Encasements are placed on both the mattress and the box spring.
- ClimbUp Interceptors are placed on all legs.
- No part of the bed is in contact with any wall.
- No bed linens, including the bed skirt, are in contact with the floor or walls.
- No electrical cords extend from the wall to the bed.

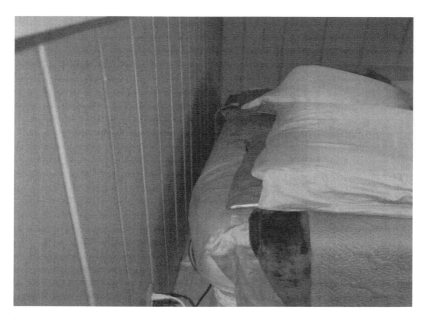

Make sure your bed does not make contact with a wall. One to two inches of space from the wall is sufficient.

The Wrong Way

Note that the mattress pictured above is in contact with the wall, which makes it easy for bedbugs to climb onto the bed.

CHAPTER 4

Products and Treatments Available to You

Mattress Encasements

- Make sure the encasements have some kind of documentation that says they are bedbug-proof, certified, or approved.
- Get the best quality you can afford.
- Make sure the encasement has a zipper. We recommend using duct tape over the zipper for added insurance.
- Get encasements for both your mattress and the box spring.

ClimbUp Interceptors

Get one interceptor for each frame leg. If your frame has six legs, get six ClimbUp Interceptors. Headboard legs need them, too. If you don't place an interceptor on each leg, bedbugs can—and will—crawl up unprotected legs.

Portable Heating Chambers

Another useful product is a portable heating chamber. There are many options to choose from, and they range in size and price. Two good brands are PackTite and ZappBug.

Other Products to Consider

Other products—for population management, *not* eradication—are steamers (for furniture, cracks, and crevices), food-grade diatomaceous earth (for cracks, crevices, and the like), and rubbing alcohol, which should be applied with a spray bottle (for luggage and nondryer items). You should not use over-the-counter sprays, foggers, or bombs. These products may kill some bedbugs, but generally they only irritate the bugs and spread them out for a while. The bugs will come back, and they will be hungry!

Where Can You Find These Products?

To find these products, you can search the Internet for bedbug products, bedbug encasements, or ClimbUp Interceptors. Additionally, most mattress stores and the following retailers will likely have some selection of bedbug products:

- Amazon.com
- Bed Bath & Beyond
- BedBug Supply.com

Professional Treatment Options

The goal of this section is to give you an idea of how each treatment works and the impact it will have on your daily life during the process. For a more detailed explanation of what is involved, contact a pest-control professional. These professionals will explain what they will do and what will be required of you.

Be advised that while there are do-it-yourself methods, we recommend having a licensed pest-control operator perform the extermination.

This is a battle of the species. The more you participate in the partnership with your exterminator, the more successful you and the exterminator will be. Teamwork wins.

Fumigation

During fumigation, your house will be tented and gassed for approximately three days. Fumigation kills all living creatures and eggs. This treatment process is similar to the process used to kill termites, but the dosage used is stronger. Typically you will be out of your home for three to four days, so you will need to find lodgings during the treatment.

Heat Treatment

Heat treatment is a one-day, nontoxic treatment. The rooms to be treated are insulated to retain the heat. The goal is to get the temperature above 130 degrees in the cubic space for a period of time because the bugs die at 122 degrees Fahrenheit. This process dehydrates the bugs and their eggs.

Chemical Spray

Chemical spraying requires a minimum of two treatments, but it generally requires three. The spray treatments are spread out over a couple of weeks because the chemicals used affect the nervous system of crawling bugs, not their eggs. Hence, the exterminator needs to wait approximately seven to ten days between treatments for the eggs to hatch. Once the eggs have hatched, the chemicals can kill the crawling bugs.

This method takes between two and three weeks to complete. On the day of the treatment, you will need to be out of the home for a period of time, normally four to eight hours. Your exterminator will inform you when you can reenter your home on the day of the treatment.

Do-It-Yourself Methods

Physical removal of infested objects is not guaranteed to get rid of all bedbugs. Remember, anything you remove should be wrapped up before you transport it outside of the infested area.

Do not use over-the-counter sprays, foggers, or bombs. These products may kill some bedbugs, but generally they only irritate the bugs and spread them out for a while. The bugs will come back, and they will be hungry!

Dry heat is your best friend. Anything you can put in the dryer should be put in the dryer. Dry items on high heat for one hour. Put larger items or items that cannot go in the dryer in large black plastic bags and put them in storage, away from the living areas, for at least five months. Another option for items too large for the dryer is to put them in your vehicle in black plastic bags, roll up the windows, and park the vehicle in the sun for the day. Please be advised that the interior of the vehicle will need to get to at least 130 degrees for this to work. Use of a thermomoter is advisable.

Made in the USA
San Bernardino, CA
25 April 2015